THIS JOURNAL BELONGS TO

A HERO? WHO, ME?
YES, YOU!

YOU are a hero on a hero's journey, and it is high time you realized it!

The hero's journey describes the soulful way you and your fellow humans are fundamentally wired. It contains the blueprint of who we are, where we're headed, and what to expect as we travel our noble path of transformation.

The concept of the hero's journey is credited to Joseph Campbell, a twentieth-century scholar who dedicated his life to studying the myths, fairytales, and origin stories of cultures around the world. In his research, he found a single story that is woven through every culture since the beginning of recorded history. That story, according to Campbell, is *The Hero's Journey*.

WHAT IS THE HERO'S JOURNEY?

In a nutshell, the hero's journey begins with an ordinary person who gets called to an extraordinary adventure. The hero (who has no idea they are a hero) finds a mentor, survives the road of trials, experiences a dark night of the soul, faces a death-defying battle, overcomes their deepest fear, gains an insight, and brings their new-found wisdom (aka elixir) home to share with his/her people.

This story was often told with a male protagonist, but it is just as much a female story. In fact, if you're a woman, you can think of your story as the *Shero's Journey*. Either way you spell it, we need this story. It inspires us, strengthens us, gives us hope, and shows us the way. Just as twelve-step programs lay out the steps to recovery (and it works if you work it), the hero's journey sets out twelve stages to recovering our power and discovering the truth of who we are.

There are four primary stages of the hero's journey: The Call, The Quest, The Reward and The Return. These are broken down into sub-phases which make up the twelve stages of the journey.

THE CALL

1. Ordinary World
2. Call to Adventure
3. Refusal of the Call
4. Meeting the Mentor

THE QUEST

5. Crossing the Threshold
6. Belly of the Whale
7. Road of Trials
8. Supreme Ordeal

THE REWARD

9. Reward

THE RETURN

10. Journey Back
11. Resurrection
12. Return with the Elixir

Accept the fact that you are currently — RIGHT NOW — at some stage of your personal hero's journey. By virtue of the fact that you are breathing, and are here reading this on planet Earth, having chosen a three-dimensional body in which to explore this brave new world, you have already said *yes* to the journey. Pat yourself on the back, even when it's up against a wall, and tell yourself throughout the day: ***I am a hero on a hero's journey!***

The difference between the hero and the ordinary you is the ordinary version gets caught in the mundane and forgets to recognize the big picture and that there is something higher going on. Thus, it is easily swayed or distracted from their noble path. The hero version of you is connected to the world of dreams, committed to awakening, dedicates your journey to something higher, and thus, doesn't give up when challenged.

Don't worry. We all weave in and out of both versions. Once you are aware that you are a hero on a hero's journey, you become more awakened minute by minute, dream by dream, day by day, one baby step and quantum leap at a time.

HOW DREAMS WEAVE INTO THE HERO'S JOURNEY

The hero's journey is not just a GPS to empower our waking lives, but one that maps the transformational potential of dreamwork. Here's how:

1. Regardless of race, politics, age, gender, sexual preference, or religion, we all dream every night, and there is a hero in all of us.

2. Dreams take place within your internal 'special world' where the rules of your waking reality are turned upside down.

3. Dreams and the hero's journey speak the language of symbols. As you become fluent in this language, you become empowered, filled with creativity, and your intuition/navigational prowess is amplified.

4. There is a direct connection between the dreams you remember upon awakening in the morning and the stage of the hero's journey you happen to be on.

5. Dreams and the hero's journey are woven into our deep unconscious

and when you pay attention to them, you are, in effect, feeding and nurturing your soul.

6. Dreams and the hero's journey ennoble our challenges, helping us find the higher purpose in our common struggles. This quickens our transformation.

7. Dreams and the hero's journey provide a lens, a frame, a context to help us shift our identity from victim to victor.

8. When we shine the light of our conscious awareness on our dreams and/or our hero's journey, we build our awakening muscles.

9. Dreams and the hero's journey are happening, beneath the surface, providing guidance, clues, and helpful insight, whether we are conscious of them or not. The more conscious we can become, the more powerful our mastery in both the dreaming and waking world.

10. If we let them, both dreams and the hero's Journey will take us on a ride through the special world and deliver us back home to the ordinary world with an elixir to share that can positively benefit the world.

HOW TO WORK WITH THIS JOURNAL

BEFORE BED
Journal about the highlights and insights gleaned from your day. Ask yourself:

- What did today teach me?

- What am I most grateful for today?

- Was there a situation that I would do over if this were a lucid dream? If so, how would I do it? What result do I imagine this would create?

- Did I see traces of my dream today? If so, what, where, how, when?

- Did I experience any synchronicities or magical occurrences? If so, what?

- Based on what's coming up for me tomorrow, what kind of dream incubation do I want to do (e.g. meditation on something you want to experience, heal or reveal in your waking life)

Pick a *Hero's Journey Dream Oracle Card* and ask yourself:

- What feelings/thoughts/insights does the message or image inspire/ignite in me?

UPON AWAKENING

In the morning, before you do anything else, start your day by:

- Recording your dream in your *Hero's Journey Dream Journal*

- Include your hunches and insights about what it means and what its wisdom is trying to get you to see/do/be

- Select a *Hero's Journey Dream Oracle* card for additional insight on what your dream is helping you with

- Meditate on the message and the card image for five to fifteen minutes

- Keep your journal open during your meditation so you can write down your insights

SYNCHRONICITY ALERT

As you move through your day, keep your journal handy so you can take note of synchronicities related to your dream, the card, or both.

ADDITIONAL JOURNALING PROMPTS

- What stage of the hero's journey am I on now? How do I feel about this?

- What dream element do I want to carry throughout the day? Why?

- What's important for me to pay attention to right now?

- What is in my blind spot?

- What should I focus on today?

- What is my message for the day?

- What is the gift/blessing/lesson in the situation I'm in right now?

- What do I need to become aware of in order to thrive in my creative endeavors/relationships/health/finances/spirituality?

MY PRAYER FOR YOU

May this journal be your best friend, witness, therapist, coach, guru, receptacle of alchemy for your fears, hall of mirrors for your strengths, and trusty traveling companion along your hero's dream journey. May this journal be a space for you to release all clouds of doubt (feel free to vent here, not just write the pretty stuff), so the sunlight of your higher awareness has a place to beam, unencumbered. May you realize, when you get to the last page (or sooner) how truly precious, loved, genius, special, dreamy and heroic you are. May your hero's journey be magnificent and may all your wildest and most wonderful dreams come true!

A-men. A-women. A-hero. A-dreams!

Kelly

THE HERO'S JOURNEY

STAGE ONE - THE ORDINARY WORLD

The journey begins with you, the hero in the ordinary world, going about business as usual, except you are unsettled. It's wise to use this stage to prepare for what is to come – psychologically and spiritually. You can pack your bags, make room in your schedule, say goodbye to unhealthy relationships, and/or attune to your nighttime dreams and the synchronistic messages you receive by day. This stage is about preparation, getting grounded and down to basics, and being grateful for the simple things in your familiar habitat that you might normally take for granted. This stage could be overlooked as not being a stage at all. *Oh, but it is!*

STAGE TWO - CALL TO ADVENTURE

This stage of the journey is about the invitation to adventure. It evokes the saying, "Many are called but few answer." Your escapade might come as a creative project, relationship, job, or workout routine, to give but a few examples. Pay attention to the action your life (including your dreams) is calling/inspiring you to do.

STAGE THREE - REFUSAL OF THE CALL

Resistance is something all heroes experience throughout their journey. You can address your foot-dragging unwillingness unconsciously with passive-aggressive behavior, sabotage mechanisms, or good old-fashioned rebellion. Or, you can tackle it consciously. Just like any shadow, when you shine your love on resistance, it loses its power. With awareness, resistance can transform and fuel your passion for becoming a masterful quester with a dreamy waking life to show for it. Keep in mind that your reluctance is often due to a conflict with your role in ordinary life. The ordinary mindset gets caught in the *thick of thin things*, whereas your heroic aspect is attuned to what's most important, even if it is inconvenient. The hero within always asks the universe, "What is life's best use for me right now?"

STAGE FOUR - MEETING THE MENTOR

This stage encourages you to accept support from the world around you. It is a sign of strength, not weakness, to have a support system, mastermind group, best friend, therapist, teacher, or reliable someone who sees you, believes in you, props you up and holds you accountable to becoming the hero you were born to be. Working with a mentor, from this or the supernatural world, can make all the difference to your hero's journey. In even your roughest moments, they remind you that the answers you seek are within. Your mentor can be someone you regularly connect with in person, on the phone, or via computer. They could also be non-physical (an angel, departed loved one or spirit guide) who you can meet in dreams. Call on your mentor to help you navigate the challenges you face as you become your most heroic self.

STAGE FIVE - CROSSING THE THRESHOLD

It is time to cross the line that separates the ordinary from the extraordinary world. In this stage, you move from the mundane to the mysterious and discover your will, your passion, and how to outsmart the threshold guardian that stands on the bridge between worlds. The guardian might pose a riddle in the form of a dream you must decode before you can pass to the sacred realm. Decode your dreams, even when they seem the most nonsensical, and you will mysteriously find yourself on the other side of challenge with an unexpected insight to empower you and carry you through your hero's journey.

STAGE SIX - BELLY OF THE WHALE

Having crossed the threshold, you are now awake to a whole new world
It is time to release your ordinary way of seeing so you can take on new
sight and perceive the special world. If challenging circumstances recently
swallowed you whole or you have had a difficult nighttime dream, welcome
to the belly of the whale! You may feel like you've been abandoned but be
assured this is not the case. The dark night of the soul (a period of sudden
darkness when your usual tips and tricks for staying afloat do not work) can
be an enormous blessing. The hero within knows that once nightmares are
worked with, they always bring oceanic power to the dreamer. Journaling
can help you drop into your depth, anchor in stillness, and find peace and
calm in your deep waters, so you can emerge from this experience stronger,
wiser, and more powerful than you ever dreamed possible.

STAGE SEVEN - ROAD OF TRIALS

During this stage you will encounter the perfect conditions for growth and
learning. Trials, challenges, and enemies will test your mettle. Allies will
step forward to hear your dreams and offer support. On the road of trials,
you will face tribulation, cement friendships, question your sense of being
and reclaim your authentic self. Your dreams have the job of delivering you
back to wholeness. Whatever happens in your waking or dreaming life will
help you release unhelpful baggage and embrace more of the power you've
disowned. Everyone and everything in your dreams, from the wild to the
tame, is an aspect of you. An enemy is your inner critic, an ally depicts
traits you have already embraced, and tests are opportunities to flex your
enlightenment muscles, so you can fearlessly journey and become the hero
you were born to be – in dreams and the waking world.

STAGE EIGHT - SUPREME ORDEAL

It is time to put all you've learned to the test. This stage brings the opportunity to own your power and alchemize your biggest challenges into blessings for you and all influenced by you. The supreme ordeal (aka the supreme opportunity) requires you to call back your power. This stage is also a reminder that life is, as Charles Swindoll says, "Ten percent what happens to you, and ninety percent how you react to it." A nightmare is an unfinished dream. When you realize your ability to direct your dreams, overcome your fear or limitation, and emerge exalted, the nightmare will have no reason to repeat! The cycle can stop, and you can move forward. Journaling can help you transform an ordeal into fuel for awakening.

STAGE NINE - REWARD

The moment you've been working and waiting for has arrived! Your power is no longer locked in a dungeon or held captive by a dragon. It is yours and you have conscious access to it. Breathe as you integrate this power, strength, beauty, wildness, fierce love, and passion back into your heart and soul. Don't leave home (or bed) without it! Consider that every situation in your life and every dream — from the seemingly benign to the technicolored drama — is encoded with soul juice and power. This is a moment to revel in. Breathe deeply as you awaken to your magnificence. Realize that YOU are the prize, and revel in the view from the summit you've worked so hard to climb.

STAGE TEN - JOURNEY BACK

Any journey, whether it be of the waking or dream variety, contains knowledge, experience and expansion. Humans are communal creatures, and have a primal desire to fit in. And yet, you've changed. You are not the same person who embarked upon this journey. Journaling at this stage will help you bypass the snipers on the road as you bring your wisdom home. On the journey back you will orient, integrate, and ground what you've learned so you don't come home looking for approval, but as a bearer of gifts.

STAGE ELEVEN – RESURRECTION

There is a symbolic reason the resurrection of the Christ happened three days after the crucifixion. The three days represents the time it takes to reorganize, reorient, and reenter as the new and improved version of yourself. The resurrection stage can best be understood as the caterpillar becoming the butterfly. There is a process, and it doesn't happen overnight. By embarking on the hero's quest, you have allowed yourself to die to your previous identity. Additionally, this stage encourages you to awaken anew and realize your transformation is not just for you, but for everyone, everywhere, especially the folks awaiting your arrival back home in the ordinary world.

STAGE TWELVE – RETURN WITH THE ELIXIR

Every time you reflect upon your time in the special world, on your hero's journey or on a significant image from a nighttime dream, it's as if you are drinking from a canteen filled with life-giving soul elixir from the extraordinary world. Record your experiences and wisdom in your journal. When you share your experience of the special world, you are passing along a soul-filled gift. We never know when a shared story will have a medicinal effect, not only on the person we share it with, but rippling on to those they influence, and so on and so on. Let this stage remind you that, "As you are lifted, all are lifted."

What is your true calling in life? What special gifts have you been given? What is the unique niche that only you can inhabit? What situations bring out your bliss? What do you typically get complimented on and shrug off because it comes so naturally? These important questions can help you recognize what Aristotle called entelechy – the great, one-of-a-kind potential you've been encoded with. Aristotle also said, "Entelechy is when the soul is actualized in the body."

The sum-total of all the outward guidance in the world doesn't hold a candle to the wisdom of the guiding force within you. Remember you're at one with the One. Open your heart to the Divine within you, then open this journal, grab a pen and allow your inner wisdom to pour through. When you open your mouth to speak, allow this higher perspective to express through you.

As you do this, may you become an awakened version of yourself. May you realize you are surrounded with more love, wisdom, beauty, healing and creative energy than you could ever fathom. May you remember you live in a beautiful world, that you are precious, and that all your dreams are sacred to the One who dreamed you into being. May you become so fluent in the language of your dreams that you co-create the most heavenly life for yourself and all beings you encounter. May your hero's journey and your wildest and most wonderful dreams all come true!

"This fateful region of both treasure and danger may be variously represented: as a distant land, a forest, a kingdom underground, beneath the waves, or above the sky, a secret island, lofty mountaintop, or profound dream state; but it is always a place of strangely fluid and polymorphous beings, unimaginable torments, superhuman deeds, and impossible delight. The hero can go forth of his own volition to accomplish the adventure, as did Theseus when he arrived in his father's city, Athens, and heard the horrible history of the Minotaur; or he may be carried of sent abroad by some benign or malignant agent, as was Odysseus, driven about the Mediterranean by the winds of the angered god Poseidon. The adventure may begin as a mere blunder, as did that of the princess of the fairy tale; or still again, one may be only casually strolling, when some passing phenomenon catches the wandering eye and lures one away from the frequented paths of man."

— JOSEPH CAMPBELL

The hero within you is dedicated to a noble cause and senses something higher is orchestrating the journey. The hero derives meaning from challenge and this gives him/ her the strength to keep putting one foot in front of the other, in dedication to something greater than themselves.

When in doubt, the hero within always asks,
"What is life's best use for me right now?"

Take time to remember, shine a light, and decode your dreams, even when they seem the most non-sensical, and you will mysteriously find yourself with unexpected insight to empower your life.

*"And the day came when the wish to remain tight in a bud
was more painful than the risk it took to blossom."*
— ANAIS NIN

Breathe deeply as you awaken to your magnificence.
Realize that YOU are the prize you've been seeking.

Affirm: With each new breath, I open the portals of my heart, mind, body and soul to align with the highest guidance available.

The hero's journey, just like dreams, speaks the language of symbols.
When you become fluent in this strange but beautiful language, you
will find yourself awakening to a most dreamy life.

Behind the clouds of doubt your inner radiance shines at its full wattage.

You can run, but you can't hide from the glory of your true nature.

"The deep unconscious contains a map of each person's authentic and heroic journey. We need only to find how to unfold and read the map."

– LAUREN Z. SCHNEIDER

You have accomplished a great deal. But, can you accept the blessings that are born of your hard work?

You are at one with the sun – the light that lights up the world!

*Feel the thrill of the winds of change blowing through your hair, as adventure
whispers from around the corner, summoning you to your next highest yet to be.*

*Feel the gentle tap on your shoulder, notice the golden ticket
in your hand, and see the red carpet rolled out before you
and leading to your highest destiny. You have been cordially
invited to show up to the party with your unique gifts,
talents, experience, perspective, joy, humor, and sense of
adventure. You are an honored guest on this journey.*

Affirm: I release all that no longer serves me,
so a better version of me can emerge.

You are attuned to the music of your soul, and what was once a still, small voice has become the loudest sound you hear.

*The sweet sound of higher ground resounds throughout your being –
so make room in your life for grace to take place, for the call of your
highest destiny to be heard, honored, and acted upon.*

It is no accident that you are on this planet, at this time, in this place, with these people. It's no accident you've been endowed with these unique gifts, talents, and life experience. It's not your job to know how your life is meant to unfold. It is only your job to be attuned to the promptings of your highest self.

Affirm: I follow breadcrumbs of bliss that lead me,
step by step, toward a most fulfilling life.

"Your Authentic Self has never been nor can be hurt, harmed, or endangered."
– MICHAEL BECKWITH

If you face a challenge, change the scene in your private meditation (or in the privacy of your journal) to the way you most wish it would be played out. Life is a dream and you are the writer, director, and wardrobe consultant. Thus, you can rewrite a scene in a way that is truly satisfying to your soul. As you practice directing your dreams, you will realize you can also direct your life.

Pack lightly. Bring only the most essential so you can be free to embrace each new moment with wide-open arms, heart, mind, body, and soul.

Affirm: I trust my 'yes' to lead me to the perfect people, places and opportunities.

It is time to open your heart, breathe deeply, and receive blessings knowing this journey is not just about or for you, but one you take on behalf of all humanity.

Make room in your world, your mind, and your heart for success, happiness, prosperity and brilliant ideas to swoop in and embrace you unencumbered.

Affirm: Divine discernment lets me know when to go, when to stop, and when to drop into the spaces in between.

"It is by going down into the abyss that we recover the treasures of life.
Where you stumble, there lies your treasure."

– JOSEPH CAMPBELL

Allow yourself to be pliant yet taut, nimble yet audacious, so the universe may move through you and delight in your rapturous self-expression.

*Your highest destiny is calling, and it may be taking you to places
within your body, mind, and soul that you never knew existed.*

Affirm: I move when moved, until then, I revel in the deliciousness of the present moment.

Before you were born, you joyously raised your hand and stood on your tippy toes to volunteer to partake in this human incarnation. Your soul smiled wildly as you traveled from the angelic realm where all is love, whole, and perfect, into the third dimension where it is, shall we say, challenging. But to bridge heaven and earth, all you must do is remember to remember who you are and from whence you came!

When you honor your dreams, your inner guidance, and the promptings of your soul, you are rewarded every step of the way with a resurgence of bliss.

Affirm: This is a journey not a sprint, so I build in breaks and reward myself along the way.

"I have been a seeker and I still am, but I stopped asking the books and the stars. I started listening to the teaching of my soul."

— RUMI

You have a circle of supernatural support, spirit guides, and angelic beings surrounding you always. You have at least ten thousand angels on hand at all times, above, beneath, and on either side of you. When you become aware of them, their support and strength can be experienced more tangibly.

Affirm: I am cradled in a supernatural web of light and
miracles that propel me along my quest.

When in doubt, consider what your highest-self would do. Ask yourself,
"If I were enlightened, what would I be, do, and how would I do it?"

*You are a celestial being, woven of starlight throughout the
galaxy of your cells, molecules, and atoms.*

Your life is not a problem to be solved, but a magical treasure hunt to explore.

Affirm: I stand in the interstellar spotlight of my life,
fully revealing my star attributes.

From a quantum field perspective, there is only one of us here. Your guides, inner and outer, are all part of the sea of brilliance in which you swim.

You are drenched with higher guidance and if you choose you can trust it to lead you to a most dreamy life.

Journal about an issue in your life where you'd like the support and guidance of the Divine. Allow wisdom to flow through you and onto the page.

Affirm: I trust the wisdom of my higher self, and follow it,
step by step, toward higher ground.

There is a yearning in your soul to move toward your highest destiny. So, what is it? What seed is gestating, urging, and burgeoning inside you? Dig past layers of ego topsoil, societal conditioning, and shoulds, and you will find your soul blueprint, awaiting your attention so it can guide you toward your most magnificent expression.

You are alive with infinite possibilities. Every cell of your body sings and shouts a full throttled YES to life!

Affirm: I celebrate each twirl, dip, and flip as I dance with
the universe in ecstatic jubilation!

Stand on the shore of the known, and feel the unfamiliar enticing you,
just over the horizon, toward the glimmer of the unknown.

You've said yes to becoming all you can be, yes to becoming your best self, and yes to contributing to the world by remembering your dreams. The universe has heard you and is responding in kind.

Even when we are near the finale of a hero's journey,
having a beginner's mind will always serve us well.

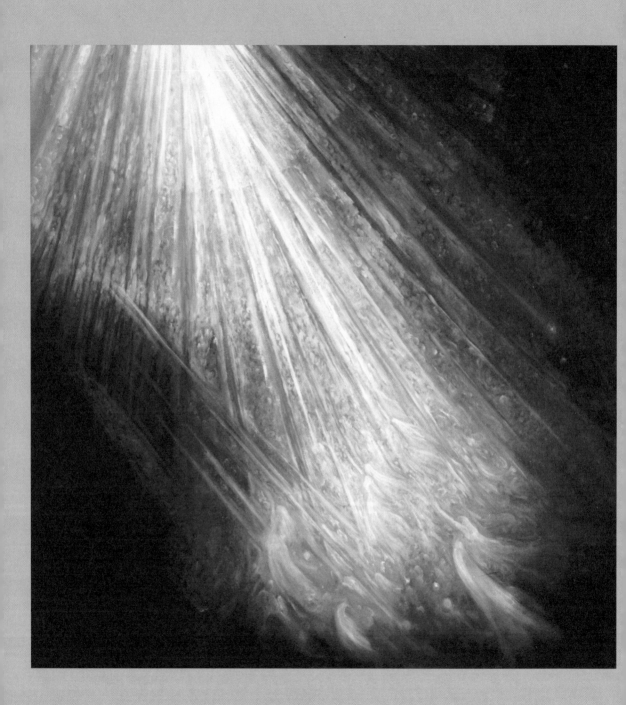

Affirm: I am exhilarated as I leap into the wild Divine!

Your charge is to enlarge! Your mandate is to become a heart space so large that all the world can fit within it, i.e. all parts of you and all parts of humanity, with nothing left out.

*In ordinary life, it's instinctual to run from things that scare you,
but when you face down those fears in dreams or waking life, you
increase your personal power exponentially!*

*When the sky becomes the ground, and the ground becomes the sky,
you realize you have flipped 'reality' on its head. No matter how rigid the
belief or experience, it's just waiting for you to turn it around.*

Affirm: Everything I do moves me toward the fulfillment of my greatest dreams.

*"Plunge boldly into the thick of life, and seize it where you will,
it is always interesting."*
— JOHANN WOLFGANG VON GOETHE

You don't need throngs of people standing shoulder to shoulder with you or cheering you on to be infused with strength and inspiration. If you meet only one kindred soul on your path, consider yourself lucky. Nurture your supportive relationships and feel the blessing of these like-minded souls for their belief in you, and for the mutual blessing you bring to each other.

If a dream is challenging, remember it isn't over until you experience a triumphant conclusion. If a dream is uplifting, remember it isn't over until you've embodied its elixir and shared it with others.

Affirm: It's my dream movie, I can re-write the script if I want to.

Attend to the simple things to ensure harmonious flow in all your relationships, and you will sleep and awaken each day with a smile on your lips.

It's not just about you, but all who will benefit from your story.

Be still, knowing the ground you stand upon is holy, and the spotlight of divine love, intelligence, beauty, and creativity is on you.

Affirm: I revel in the blessings discovered in the most
unlikely people and places.

You are infinitely powerful, wise, strong, and blessed. Yet, you've only taken conscious ownership of about five percent of your natural inheritance. What a thrill to know there's more of you where this came from!

Your biggest, scariest shadow is your superpower in disguise.

Allow that which scares you to become fuel to ignite your dreams. Allow that FUEL to give you a Future *that is* Unlimited, Empowered and Lucid.

Affirm: The awareness of the preciousness of life puts a
gale force beneath my wings.

Stop, drop, sit, breathe, look around, take in the view, and acknowledge all the blessings and treasures you've learned and earned along the way.

If you think about it, you have an unending list of things for which to be grateful. In fact, if you could really see, you'd fall to your knees in absolute wonderment at the blessings in your life.

Affirm: I am an attractor beam, magnetic to the best things in life!

It is time to honor where you've been, claim your new identity,
and prepare to make a bold leap into the future you've been dreaming
of and working toward for so long.

Like the heroes before you, feel the doubt, and follow through anyway!

*When you see yourself in everyone and everything, your defenses
soften, your heart opens, and your learning curve is off the charts.*

Affirm: I open my heart to graciously behold the blessings at my feet.

How much good can you handle; how much love can you take?
How much good can you endure before your fortress breaks?
(Breaking open is a good thing, by the way!)

All events that take place in your daytime and nighttime dreams are attempts to awaken your core strengths, gifts, genius and power.

Dive into the depths of your inner ocean and discover the treasure chest that's been patiently waiting.

Affirm: Vulnerability it one of my greatest strengths.

Your higher self cradles and feeds you the guidance you need as you take each step along your sacred journey.

Remembering who you are, thus valuing who you are,
is the key to living an awakened life.

*You wake up when you consciously 're-member' (put back together)
your true identity as an infinite spiritual being, powerful beyond
measure, and heir to all the wonder this earth has to offer.*

The true you is still intact! Yes, it may be covered by layer
upon layer of protective masks, armor, or scar tissue,
but it's still there, waiting to be discovered!

Affirm: I hold the key to an awakened life of love, magic, and treasure beyond measure.

Revisit your passionate intention for this lifetime.
Remind yourself, "For this I was born!"

Feel the joy at having arrived at this moment.

The adventure of a lifetime is beckoning you now.

Affirm: I use my entire pallet to paint with broad strokes
as I participate vividly in life.

*Feel your DNA and your inner circuitry being rewired and recalibrated
toward a more expansive, yet grounded, version of yourself.*

Your story emanates through every cell of your being.

You are being summoned to something magnificent.

Affirm: I am connected with the celestial body of the universe, I have permission to shine at maximum wattage.

*Feel the butterflies and sensations of love well up within you, and
trust that saying yes to the beckoning winds will lead you to the
perfect people, places and situations for your maximum soul growth.*

Be grateful for the space between where you are and where you long to be.

Allow the diversity of life and the entire ocean of emotion of all sentient beings to be celebrated and loved.

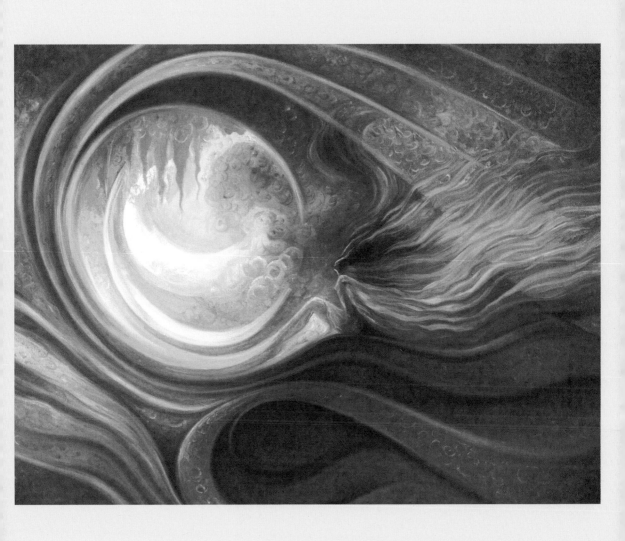

Affirm: I am high on life, and off my rocker with the overwhelming beauty that surrounds me.

Consider your emotions to be your allies, informants, and friends.
If you allow them, they will always lead to the most magnificent treasure.

In every moment you can begin anew. With this next breath,
know you can wipe the slate clean and release any baggage you've
been carrying thus far because you no longer need it.

Exhale the past completely. And as you inhale, open yourself to a whole new vista, a whole new incarnation, a whole new story of who you are and why you're here.

What if the entire world was conspiring for your greatest good?

Affirm: I open my heart and let myself be reborn, so I may revel in
a new, improved, lighter and brighter version of who I am.

Honor the whisper of your soul.

When life isn't going your way, remember that you are the director of your dreams — the ones you have at night and by day — and you can orchestrate a change of course, tactic, or whatever else is needed.

Allow yourself to feel, sense, and see genius, gently yet powerfully wrapping itself around you, lifting you higher than you ever thought you could reach.

Affirm: In the hologram of life, I already have it all,
and am already where I want to be.

Your words are seeds, planted in the fertile soil of the minds and hearts of all who are destined to be changed by your wisdom.

Stand still and explore what is worthy and noble about your shadow and how,
by embracing it, it will add fuel to your most luminous expression.

Affirm: When I share the gold of my soul with the world, the treasure is multiplied!

You are the sunlight of the spirit! There is nothing you have
ever done or will do that can diminish your light.

Look for the lesson and the blessing in every situation and you will find it.

Life is on your side and the unknown is your friend. Hear the calling, muster your courage, gather your allies, and go for it!

The higher self in everyone you interact with is rooting for your awakening.

Affirm: I am a citizen of both heaven and earth.
I soar high and land with grace.

On your hero's journey, you will travel far from home (if only in your mind) but never forget your roots, and your gratitude for all that nurtures, feeds, and grounds you.

When you reflect on your life, you will realize the most difficult challenges taught you the most valuable lessons and made you more resourceful and resilient than you would otherwise be. Revel in the reality that you are who you are today, precisely because of the challenges you've faced and aced.

Gather your energy, creativity, talent, and will, so no part is left behind as you cross a new threshold of adventure.

Affirm: The elixir of love encoded within me is
transmitted through my radiance.

Let your glow do the heavy lifting.

Honor the wisdom you've earned and learned, while honoring the people in your circle of life, by remembering that you are the elixir. Without having to say a word or do a single thing, you are the medicine, blessing and presence that soothes the hearts, minds and souls of all you meet.

Congratulations! You have a life worth celebrating! Stop and acknowledge who you've become, what you've accomplished, and the blessings you can now share with the world. Breathe this in. Soak it up, let its splendor fill you, radiate through you, and elevate your awareness, so you can share even more blessings.

Reflect upon your dreams and your hero's journey and recognize that you are more yourself now than you've ever been ... and there's more where that came from! After all, the end of one journey is the beginning of the next.

But, before you embark upon your next adventure, take a moment to acknowledge yourself for participating in this quest, for keeping your eternal flame burning bright, and honoring your purpose for being alive. At this point, you don't have to wait for others to light your fire, because the permission you need has already been granted ... by YOU! Know that true joy comes from fulfilling your pact with life, and ultimately, by being a splendid torch that lights the way for others.

KELLY SULLIVAN WALDEN